MY Rhyming BIBLE

Published by World Publishing, Inc., Grand Rapids, MI 49418

Library of Congress Catalog Card Number 96-60870

Printed in the United States of America

1 2 3 4 5 6 — 99 98 97 96

My Rhyming BIBLE

Applying Bible Stories to Little Lives

Written and Illustrated By Rob Suggs

TABLE OF CONTENTS

The Old Testament

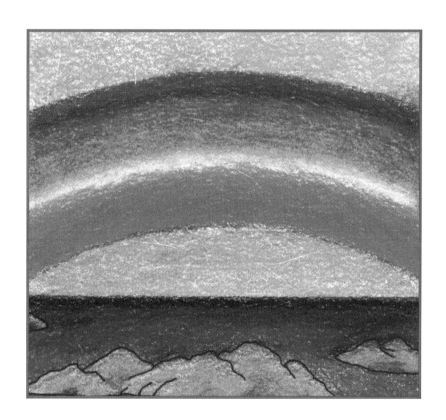

In the Beginning

On the first day the Lord said, "Let there be light";
there was sun in the day and then darkness at night.
On the second day the Lord said, "Let there be sky,"
and he colored it blue, and he put it up high.
On the third day the Lord made the land and the seas,
and he planted the flowers, and bushes and trees.

On the fourth day the Lord made the moon and the sun,
and put stars in the sky and gave light to each one.
On the fifth day the Lord made the birds and the fish,
and he told them, "be fruitful, and spread as you wish."
On the sixth day the Lord made the woman and man,
to live as his children the best way we can.
On the seventh he rested; creation was done,
and the world is our proof that God loves each one.

Genesis 1-2

Adam and Eve

When God divided night from day
and land from sea, and rock from clay,
he had a lovely world worth seeing,
so he made a human being.
Thus, the human race began
with Adam, planet Earth's first man.
No other people—Adam only;
God knew Adam would be lonely.
So he placed by Adam's side
a special mate, a friend, a bride.
Her name was Eve, and she was made
to work with Adam. She obeyed.
Man and woman, girl and boy,
God made us both to serve with joy.

Genesis 2

A Snake in the Garden

Eve and Adam
had a duty:
tend the garden
filled with beauty;
care for beasts
both wild and tame,
and give each
animal a name.
The trees were filled
with fruit to eat,
which gave them strength
and tasted sweet.
But one command
was absolute:
"Avoid this tree;
don't eat its fruit."
The Lord provided
them so much,
but this one tree
they could not touch.

And then the serpent slithered in
to introduce the world to sin.
He questioned whether God was right
and tempted Eve to take a bite.
She did, and Adam followed suit;
they'd tasted the forbidden fruit.

God knew they'd done what he'd forbidden,
so he called, but they were hidden.
Trembling in fear and shame,
they looked for someone else to blame.
God knew his children disobeyed
the wise and worthy rules he'd made.
God loved Adam still, and Eve,
but he knew their time had come to leave
the Garden, and together roam
the earth to find another home.

Genesis 3

Cain and Abel

Hear this fable: Cain and Abel.
Abel slain by brother Cain
whose sacrifice was not as nice.
The tale tells us: Don't be jealous.
Genesis 4

The Great Flood

Noah's neighbors thought him odd
because he was a man of God
who loved the laws of his Creator.
(They were sorry for it later.)
God had Noah build a boat
quite large a barge, but fit to float.
His neighbors stood around and laughed:
"Who needs a boat, canoe, or raft?"

But Noah just
ignored the crowd.
He watched, above,
a great black cloud
and calmly found
himself a crew:
a floating farm;
a cruising zoo!

From every breed,
he had a pair;
the wildest party
anywhere.
His neighbors rubbed
their eyes in wonder.
Then they heard
a clap of thunder,
felt the rain
begin to pour,
and ran for Noah's
open door!

But every room aboard was full
of bear, or boar, baboon, or bull.
The waters rose, the sky was dark;
they waved goodbye to Noah's Ark.
Obey the Lord in all you do.
Don't worry when they laugh at you
because you choose to serve the Lord.
And when it rains, come climb aboard!

Genesis 6-7

The Rainbow

For forty days the sky was dark
as Noah's family sailed the ark.
And then, at last, God stopped the rain,
and there was sun across the plain,
but all the land lay deep down under.
Noah's family had to wonder
when the ark would finally park
and when the crew could disembark.

So Noah let
a raven fly
to search for land
that might be dry.
But there was none;
it was not there.
The bird returned
to Noah's care.
But then one day,
he sent a dove
who spotted land
from high above.
The coast was clear
from east to west.
The day had come!
The ark could rest.
So family, birds,
and beasts came out
and felt the ground
and walked about.
And Noah quickly
built an altar
so their faith
might never falter.
Then, a rainbow
shined above
—a sign of God;
a sign of love.

Genesis 8

The Tower of Power

Because they wanted
fame and power,
men once tried
to build a tower.
One as high
as heaven—higher!
All the world
would soon admire
a spectacle
to gaze upon:
a monument
to block the sun.
And yet their
building plans ignored
the very Highest One:
the Lord,
who knew their pride
had grown too high
as Babel reached
into the sky.
God twisted tongues,
confused their speech;
no longer were
the stars in reach.
They tossed their tools
and left the tower,
scattering
within the hour,
leaving God
alone in power.

Genesis 11

Abraham, Abraham

Abraham, Abraham,
old as can be,
No little children
to sit on his knee.
No little children
to pull on his beard,
And too late to have them,
old Abraham feared.
Along came an angel
to visit one day,
to tell them a baby
would be on the way
and remind them that
Abraham's God is so great,
that we're never too old
and it's never too late.

Genesis 18

Abraham's Faith

Abraham had only one little boy,
and Isaac, his son, brought him nothing but joy.
He had waited so long to be blessed with a son
and he poured all his love into this special one.
But the Lord said to Abraham one awful day,
"You will make me a sacrifice.Make it this way:
You will go to the mountains and there in the wild,
you will offer a sacrifice: Isaac, your child."

So Abraham held back his tears, and he swallowed;
he left on the journey, and young Isaac followed.
They came to the place, and he lifted his knife,
but an angel called, "Abraham! Spare the boy's life!
Your faith and obedience passed such a test
that your family and children will truly be blessed.
They will shine like the stars, and will spread like the sand;
they will cover the earth and they'll bless every land."

Genesis 22

Jacob and Esau

Isaac had a pair of sons
not much like one another.
Jacob was the younger one,
and mostly stayed with Mother.
Esau was the firstborn child;
the birthright went to him.
He liked to hunt and wander wild
or fish in streams and swim.
So one day he was passing through
and felt an awful hunger.
And there, preparing beefy stew,
was Jacob, who was younger.
He begged the boy for just a share
of brother's tempting meal.
"Just sell your birthright—make me heir,"
said Jacob. "That's our deal."

And Esau quickly made the trade and had a filling dinner.
He later knew the deal he'd made left Jacob as the winner.
For Jacob went to Father's side to get the firstborn's blessing,
disguised beneath a goat's thick hide to keep his dad from guessing.
When Esau heard, he cried aloud, and swore that Jake would pay.
And Isaac wept, his old head bowed, while Jacob ran away.
Many, many years did pass before their anger died.
But one day they met upon the grass, and hugged, forgave, and cried.

Genesis 25, 27

Jacob and the Angels

Sing a song of Jacob, who was known for his deceiving;
and of God, who first believes in us, and never stops believing.
Jacob hurt his dearest ones, and had to run away;
he never would feel lonelier than he felt that day.
The sun went down; he stopped to sleep; his pillow was a stone.
He had a dream, in which it seemed he wasn't there alone.

A ladder
loomed above him,
stretching high
into the air,
and up and down
the angels climbed—
and countless ones
were there.
A voice said,
"I'm the Lord
your God,
and I am still
with you;
I'll bless
your people always,
and I'll bring you
homeward, too."
When Jacob woke,
a different man,
he gave up
all his schemes.
He knew instead
he'd trust in God,
the one who blessed
his dreams.
Genesis 28

Joseph's Coat

Jacob had twelve different sons,
of which he had two favorite ones.
By far, he loved his Joseph most,
which, sadly, made young Joseph boast.
And so as he described his dreams,
the brothers planned all kinds of schemes
until one day, Joe came to gloat
because he had a special coat.
They muttered, "Hear how Joseph brags;
he wears fine clothes and we wear rags.
Well, no more dreams will Joseph tell!"
They threw him in an empty well,

which might have been
young Joseph's grave;
instead, they sold him
as a slave.
But keeping Joseph's
fancy coat,
they went and killed
a mountain goat
whose blood upon
the coat was red,
so Jacob thought
his son was dead.
Joseph, always
spoiled and petted,
knew the truth
and he regretted
how he'd made
his brothers feel,
but now he found
that God was real.
Since God was with him,
he was brave
and quickly rose
from humble slave.

Genesis 37

Joseph in Egypt

In Egypt Joseph had to suffer, but his troubles made him tougher.
He had a gift, from God, for dreams; he understood their inner themes.
And news of this amazing thing soon reached the ears of Egypt's king.
His dream of cows both fat and leanwas puzzling him: what could it mean?
But Joseph brought the meaning out: it warned the king of years of drought.
The king was quick to realize that Joseph was both good and wise.
And so he placed him in command. The former slave now ruled the land!

Genesis 41

Baby Moses

Joseph's descendants
were slaves—every one.
And Pharaoh (the king)
said to kill each new son.
But a slave who was brave—
a courageous young mother
—sent Miriam, her daughter,
to save baby brother.
The basket he lay in
was put in the Nile,
and nearby she hid
to keep watch for a while.
And who came along
but the Pharaoh's own daughter!
She came, with a servant,
to bathe in the water
and saw, in the reeds,
a peculiar thing floating,
and found the surprise
of a baby boy boating!

Then, Miriam was happy they'd found little brother;
she offered to find them a good Hebrew mother.
So Moses' true mother was brought as a nurse.
And the family avoided the king's evil curse.
For Moses would grow to become just the man
who was chosen for God's most magnificent plan.

Exodus 1-2

The Burning Bush

Ever seen a bush in flame
that won't burn out—just stays the same?
Well, Moses saw exactly that,
and, stranger still—they had a chat!
"No closer, Moses! God's around.
Take off your shoes, it's holy ground.
The Israelites have cried to me;
they're slaves, and you will set them free."

Then Moses asked, "But who am I?
I'm weak and I'm afraid to try."
But God said, "I'll go with you there;
I AM WHO I AM everywhere."
So Moses faced the Pharaoh later,
Pharaoh was great—but God is greater!

Exodus 3

The Plagues

Moses courageously spoke for the Lord,
but the Pharaoh was stubborn and simply ignored.
But the prophet persisted: "Let God's people go!"
He predicted ten plagues; for God's power to show.
So the river turned bloody—then came thousands of toads,
which were followed by gnats, and then flies—there were loads!
The cattle of Egypt were stricken, and then,
all the people of Egypt had boils on their skin.

Then came hail, and then locusts who came to consume,
then the whole land of Egypt grew dark as a tomb!
There was one final sign of God's limitless power:
The angel of death, one particular hour,
would pass over houses whose doors had the mark,
but punish Egyptians, with death in the dark.
The doors of the Israelites showed they believed,
but the Egyptians did not, and that morning they grieved.
So Pharoah gave in, with a sigh, and agreed;
he surrendered to Moses: the slaves were all freed.

Exodus 7-12

Parting the Sea

The Israelites left
under Moses' command,
and bade Egypt farewell,
and made haste from that land.
But it wouldn't be easy:
escape would be narrow,
for they spotted behind them
the troops of the Pharaoh!
The Pharoah was taunting them,
"Go ahead--flee!
You'll never escape;
you'll be trapped by the sea!"
But Moses was faithful.
His people were brave,
for none would return
to the life of a slave.
At the Red Sea, they stopped,
asking where to go now.
There must be a way to escape--
but just how?

The chariots were coming; Egyptians were near!
The Israelites heard them, and huddled in fear.
Then God spoke to Moses, "Now stretch out your hands,
and the waters will part, and obey your command."
And the Israelites ran through the sea's special path;
the Egyptians pursued, but they felt the Lord's wrath:
as they followed, the waters returned to their place,
and the chariots were flooded, thus ending the chase.
The Israelites finally knew they were free,
for the Lord made a way when he parted the sea.

Exodus 14

God Provides

God used a cloud to lead them through the day.
He sent a fiery pillar every night.
And Bread fell on the sand,
as they sought the Promised Land,
for God took care of every Israelite.

Exodus 13, 16

The Ten Commandments

The Lord gave Moses ten commands
that every person understands.
Just count them using both your hands:

"I am your God, no others reign.
From idol-making you'll refrain.
Respect my name each time you speak,
and keep the sabbath every week.
Obey your father and your mother.
Never, never kill another.
Respect all marriage, and be true.
Don't steal; it won't belong to you.
Be honest never tell a lie.
Don't long for others' things nearby."

Obey these laws and never cease;
they'll bring your life success and peace.

Exodus 20

The Ten Spies

Those people called the Israelites
once traveled many days and nights
through lonely hills and desert sand
to find the lovely Promised Land
where grass was green and days were sunny
—overflowing milk and honey.
Moses brought them to the border.
Then he called the tribes to order,
asking for a dozen spiesto scout the land
and then advise the Israelites
on what to do, and whether they
could travel through.

The spies went in,
and then returned,
reporting all that
they had learned.
The first report
came from the ten
who said, "We can't
go there and win!
The men are giants—
we'd be killed."
But two were stubborn:
they were thrilled
with lovely fruit
and fertile lands
—and God would put it
in their hands.
So two said, "yes,"
and ten said "no";
ten said "stay,"
and two said, "go."

So Moses prayed
to God alone
then told them,
in a weary tone,
"With all we've seen,
I find it odd
that still, you're lacking
faith in God.
In trusting his
almighty hand,
we're strong enough
for any land.
He wanted you
to have this home,
but, since you don't
believe, you'll roam."

For forty weary
years they wandered
in the desert,
and they pondered:
Happiness is
trusting him;
but doubt and fear,
make living grim.
Numbers 13-14

The Walls of Jericho

Of all the places they could go
the Israelites feared Jericho!
The walls were thick, the towers tall;
it seemed the city couldn't fall.
But God moves in mysterious ways.
He said, "We'll win in seven days!
For six, you'll march around in line,
with priests in front, to show you're mine.
And on the seventh—seven laps:
when trumpets blow, the walls collapse."

For six long days, and even nights,
the city guards watched Israelites
march in a circular parade;
an army small, but not afraid.
And then, upon the seventh morn,
each priest of God blew on his horn
all the city heard the sound
as walls came tumbling to the ground!
Every tower lay in dust;
because the people placed their trust
in God, who has a greater power
than the strongest, highest tower.

Joshua 3, 6

Gideon's Army

The Israelites suffered from many invaders
who plundered their land and their crops, using raiders.
And some of the worst were their neighbors in Midian.
God sent a leader: a farmer named Gideon.
Calling the people, he told them, "It's time
that we deal with these neighbors and punish their crime."
So they went to the hills, and he said, "Now we've found them.
From hilltops above we completely surround them.
We have fewer soldiers, but, if you're afraid,
you should leave us right now, and not come on the raid."

The Israelites listened to Gideon's words,
and some of them quit: an amazing two thirds.
Not for a moment did Gideon's heart sink,
and he sent some more home when the men took a drink,
saying, "Men who will put their whole face in the water
are careless; such troops would be in for a slaughter.
But those who scoop water with eyes on the field
are the ones who can carry our sword and our shield."

From thirty-two thousand, three hundred remained.
You or I might surrender, but Gideon refrained.
And he ordered his men to put torches in jars,
as they waited for darkness and silence and stars.
And they smashed all the jars and ran down the hills screaming.
The slumbering Midianites thought they were dreaming.
The smallest of armies was perfectly strong;
they defeated a larger, more powerful throng.
Midian suffered defeat in its slumbers,
for strength is in God, not in weapons or numbers.

Judges 6-7

Strong Man

Samson was born to be handsome and strong
and watch over the Israelites all his life long.
Their Philistine enemies knew it and frowned:
for they couldn't attack with Samson around.
With his hands Sam fought lions and every wild beast
there was nothing, or no one, that scared him the least.
But the enemy plotted and planned to deceive,
and they had one more trick up their Philistine sleeve.
For they knew one Delilah, a Philistine beauty,
and trained the young lady for Philistine duty.
She took up with Samson and used all her charm;
he never suspected she meant any harm.
She begged him to tell her his secret of strength,
and he told her of bowstrings in seven new lengths.
If ever, he claimed, he were tied with such cord,
he'd be weak as a kitten, not strong in the Lord.
He dropped off to sleep, as she chuckled inside,
and when Samson awoke—well, he found himself tied.
But he broke all the bowstrings with simply a shrug,
and he laughed as he gave his Delilah a hug.

But Delilah kept asking, and kept up her hopes,
as he offered false answers, like seven new ropes.
But whenever she put his claims to the test,
he would still be as strong when he woke from his rest.
So she cried and she pouted and threatened to go,
until Samson revealed what she wanted to know.
"The secret, my honey? It lies in my hair,
I would lose all my power if that were not there."
He fell asleep and dozed until dawn;
when he woke he discovered his strength was all gone.
The Philistines came and imprisoned their prize,
and they chained him, and mocked him, and blinded his eyes.

He was put on display in the Philistine temple.
He wept as he prayed, and his prayer was quite simple:
"Remember me, Lord, though I did forget you,
and allow me the strength for one task I must do."
So he straightened his back on a Philistine pillar,
and was, once again, the old Philistine killer.
He pulled down the roof with his last dying breath,
and he sent all his foes to a Philistine death.
He'd been given a gift, but he treated it wrong;
in the end we are weak, for it's God that is strong.

Judges 13-16

Loyal Ruth

Ruth was a woman who lived far away
and, sadly, became a young widow one day.
Naomi, her mother-in-law, feeling quite low
told her, "Ruth, to the home of your husband you'll go,
and you'll make a new home with those women and men,
and you'll start a new life, even marry again."
But her daughter-in-law said, "Oh, no! Can't you see?
My Naomi, wherever you are, I shall be.
Where you go, I will go; where you stay, I will stay,
and your people and God will be mine every day."

Naomi knew just what the young woman meant,
so together to Bethlehem both of them went.
They made the long journey, crossing the plain,
and started to work in a field picking grain
where the owner, named Boaz, began to watch Ruth;
he saw in her beauty, her wisdom, her truth.
So they married, and Ruth made his household quite homey,
but honored and cared for her great friend, Naomi.

The Book of Ruth

God Hears Hannah's Prayer

Hannah wanted very much a child to call her own.
She prayed so hard and cried and such, the priest could hear her moan.
His name was Eli; and he had a message from above:
"You need not be so very sad, for God will show his love."
And, yes, she had a little boy–the Lord had heard and blessed.
The man and wife were filled with joybut brought a firm request:
"Our little Samuel surely camefrom God–it's just that simple.
Dedicate him to God's name and train him in the temple."

1 Samuel 1

A Voice in the Night

Samuel grew as he trained in the temple,
with Eli, his teacher.
Their lifestyle was simple.
But one night somebody was calling his name;
through the darkness the voice, and a mystery came.

He ran to old Eli and said, "Did you call?"
But the priest answered, "No, you just dreamed it, that's all."
The voice spoke once more as the boy turned in,
calling, "Samuel! Samuel!" Yes, once again.
He ran back to Eli, but Eli said, "No."
He had not said a word, and he told the boy so.
But a third time the boy heard the voice gently speak;
and again he sought Eli. Who else could he seek?

But the priest had a thought. He explained it this way:
"If you hear it again, I advise you to say,
'I am listening Lord, it is you I have heard,
and I'm eager and willing to hear every word.'"
Old Eli was right; though the night had been odd,
little Samuel was hearing none other than God,
who delivered a message of wonderful things,
for the boy would bless Israel, anointing its kings.
So Eli raised Samuel as prophet and priest.
He grew in the Lord, and his wisdom increased.

1 Samuel 3

David and the Giant

Among all the enemies Israelites cursed,
the Philistines certainly stood as the worst.
They were led by Goliath, a towering giant,
who stood at the border and dared them, defiant.
He terrified Israel—his height was nine feet—
an opponent no Israelite wanted to meet.
"Just send me a warrior," Goliath would call,
"and my men will surrender if only I fall!"
The Israelites trembled, and none had the heart;
they were certain the giant would tear them apart.

But a shepherd boy, David, whose brothers were there,
was disgusted that no one would take such a dare.
"I may be a boy, but I've killed bear and lion.
Our strength is from God, who's the Lord of all Zion."
So he picked up five stones that he found in a brook;
His pouch, sling and stones were all that he took.
When Goliath saw David, he laughed and he taunted:
"So this is the Israelite warrior I wanted!
You think I'm a dog you can fight with a stick?
Or is it a pitiful Israelite trick?"

But the boy said, "you carry the strength of the sword,
but I come to you now in the name of the Lord!"
He ran to the giant and pulled out his sling,
and he put in a stone and he gave it a fling!
The stone hit the giant, he falleth, he dieth,
and that was the end of the giant Goliath.
For David was small and the Philistine tall,
but the bigger they come—well, the harder they fall.

1 Samuel 17

David the King

One day David's fame was nearly zero;
next he was the nation's greatest hero.
David killed the giant, after all,
and only one was jealous: it was Saul.
The King resented David's newfound fame,
for all of Israel knew the shepherd's name.
"Hail to David!" all the people said;
the King, however, wanted David dead.
He saw the boy and hurled a deadly spear,
but missed, and David ran and hid in fear.
But David had a friend, a special one:

He spoke up for his friend throughout the strife,
and, more than once, he saved young David's life.
The shepherd boy was not the one to fall,
for in the end, the one who fell was Saul.
He displeased God, and died with sword and shield
one day on Israel's bloody battlefield.
And David, who was young and brave and smart,
in every way the man of God's own heart,
became the king and Israel's pride and glory,
writing psalms--but that's another story!

1 Samuel 20

The Wisdom of Solomon

Solomon ruled as a king, strong and wise
for he knew what was truth, and he knew what were lies.
And two women came to him, disputing each other:
they fought for a baby; which one was the mother?
"It's mine," said the first, "and this woman has none,
so she crept in last night and she's stolen my son."
But the other said, "No! He's been mine all along!
And you're jealous of me, but you're certainly wrong!"
So the King thought a while and he called for a guard,
and he said, "Here's the answer, it's not very hard:
with one child and two mothers, we have to be fair;
cut the baby in half, and you'll each have a share."
But the first mother gasped, and she quickly cried, "No!
Give the child to the other! Don't cut him! I'll go."
And the king knew for sure who was really the one:
for that woman who cried really loved her young son.
And he gave her the baby, a wonderful prize,
and the other was punished for telling such lies.

1 Kings 3

Elijah and the Prophets

King Ahab ruled with Jezebel,
but didn't serve the Lord too well.
Their nation's faith grew rather stale
and folks began to worship Baal.
Elijah came to ask the king,
"Have you forgotten everything?
The Law of God forever stands;
you've violated his commands.
Your Baal is false, without a doubt;
So he and God will have it out!
Mount Carmel is the place we'll go
to see from Whom all blessings flow."
The word was spread through hill and dale:
a showdown! It was God or Baal.

And when they reached the mountain crest Elijah asked which god was best.
A sacrifice to each was made, and Baal went first. Their prophets prayed
and danced around their bull for hours, yet they saw no godly powers.
Elijah laughed: "Where is your god? It's quiet here; that's very odd!
Your Baal is pale—he'll fail and falter." Elijah then built another altar,
with a bull, and cried with zeal: O hear me, Lord, and show you're real!"

And fire from heaven lit the sky,
with power no one could deny.
The bull was burnt; the people fell
upon their faces, knowing well
which God was real and which was fake;
idols are a big mistake!
1 Kings 18

A Child Leader

Josiah was king as a child of just eight,
but he grew to a man who was righteous and great.
When he found that the temple was needing repair,
he insisted they fix every step, stone, and stair.
For the temple of God should be fully restored
as a worthy and wonderful house of the Lord.
As they dug in the rubble, they suddenly saw
a remarkable parchment: a book of the Law!

So they came to the palace and read it aloud,
and Josiah was moved, for he wept and he bowed
and he tore at his clothing to show that he grieved
for the goodness of God in this scroll they received.
He knew that the country was set for disaster
because it had turned from the Lord as its master.
He gathered the people to hear the scroll read,
and decreed that indeed they would do what it said.

2 Kings 22

Solomon's Temple

Solomon, wisest of all of the kings,
was to rule over Israel, achieve many things.
But of all of his works, one achievement stood tall,
for the temple of God was a beautiful hall
with a plan for its building which came from the Lord;
and the king planned it out, not a detail ignored.
From all over the world came the wood and the stone,
as the king gave his orders and watched from the throne.
When the work was completed, each level and story,
they offered it up to the Lord and his glory.

2 Chronicles 2-3

The Builder

The Israelites were once again a nation falling into sin,
so finally the time came when their country had to fall.

And sure enough, there was a war. A dark disaster was in store.
Jerusalem was great no more. Invaders smashed the wall.

The Israelites became their slaves (well, those that weren't in battle graves),
but God is good! He always saves a few to start again.

And Nehemiah, back in town, surveyed the walls that toppled down
and didn't stop to moan or frown, but gathered all the men.

"We brought upon ourselves this trouble. Now, our efforts we'll redouble
and restore from all the rubble this important wall."

So brick by brick, they used their hands, while Nehemiah gave commands
and up from dust and desert sands it stood, so proud and tall.

The Book of Nehemiah

Brave Queen Esther

In Persia the king had a search for a queen,
until all of the women had come to be seen,
and he spoke to each woman to study and test her,
and finally found a new queen: her name was Esther.
She didn't tell them that she was a Jew,
for they just might reject her—oh what could she do?
But the king did select her, a wonderful thing!
And she made a good life for herself and the king.
But the guards of the palace were hatching a plot,
they would murder the king—but the plotters were caught,
because Mordecai, cousin of Esther, could hear,
and he told cousin Esther that danger was near.

An evil man, Haman, soon came on the scene,
with more power than all but the king and the queen,
and he ordered all people to kneel down before him,
but Mordecai stubbornly chose to ignore him.
For he would just kneel to the God that was true,
and so Haman, now furious, knew what to do:
he proclaimed that the Jews could be legally killed,
and all over the kingdom, their blood might be spilled.
So Mordecai wrote to his cousin again,
of the threat to all Hebrews, both women and men.

But the Queen was quite worried of one certain thing:
by the law, she'd be killed if she went to the king,
for the law said you must be invited there first;
but she went to him anyway, fearing the worst.
The king was quite happy; his kindness impressed her.
He promised to grant any wish to Queen Esther.
She only requested the Jews to be spared,
and he asked who had threatened those people—who dared?
So Esther revealed evil Haman's decree,
and they had him arrested; the Jews would be free.
Wherever such evil can spread or can fester,
the Lord will trust someone like you—or Queen Esther.

The Book of Esther

Obeying God

A man who avoids evil people is blessed,
for the Law of the Lord is what pleases him best;
by day and by night he gives thought to its reason,
a tree by the stream bearing fruit in its season,
whose leaves never fade.
So that man has it made!

And the evil ones? They're like the dust the wind blows.
They won't stand in the place where the faithful man goes.
So the Lord watches over the righteous one's way,
but the way of the wicked will perish one day.

Psalm 1

God Cares

O Lord, our own Lord, how your name is adored.
For in all of the earth it cannot be ignored!
When I think of your heavens, the work of your hand,
and the moon and the stars, which you carefully planned,
I ask, "what is man, that you notice he's there?
And just what is a person, for whom you would care?"
For a little bit lower than angels, you placed him,
with glory and honor you crowned and you graced him,
and made him the ruler of works from your hand,
and put everything under his feet to command
from the flocks and the herds to the fish and the birds.
O Lord, our own Lord, how your name is adored.
For in all of the earth it cannot be ignored!

Psalm 8

The Heavens Praise God

The heavens are telling of God and his glory;
the skies are his handiwork, telling his story.
They're telling the tale for us day after day,
and they show what they know every night, the same way.
And wherever on earth people happen to be,
they can look to the sky; in their hearts they will see,
and they'll hear in the heavens the voice that will speak,
for it travels forever, wherever men seek.
May the words of my mouth and my heart's meditation,
be pleasing to you, O my rock and salvation.

Psalm 19

My Loving Shepherd

The Lord is my shepherd,
he fills all my needs
as I lie in green pastures
and go where he leads.
Beside pleasant waters
he sets me at rest,
and he shows me the path
that will honor him best.
Even when walking
in darkness and shade,
you will always be with me;
I'll not be afraid,
for your rod and your staff
will protect me and guide.
Though my enemies find me,
I never must hide.
Your oil soothes my head,
with my cup overflowing;
your goodness and mercy
will come where I'm going.
I'll stay all my days in
the Lord's palace glowing.

Psalm 23

No Reason to Fear

God is our hiding place; he is our power.
Providing in trouble, he's there every hour.
And fear will not find us, though earth be in motion,
and mountains fall into the heart of the ocean,
or tidal waves roar and the flood waters pour;
No, the mountains themselves cannot shake his devotion.

Psalm 46

Shout for Joy

Shout joy to the Lord,
every creature on earth,
and worship the Lord
with your gladness and mirth;
Now enter his presence
with loud joyous song
and know he is God;
we've been his all along.
Now enter his gates
with thanksgiving and praise,
for the Lord and his love
will endure all our days.
Psalm 100

Seeking God

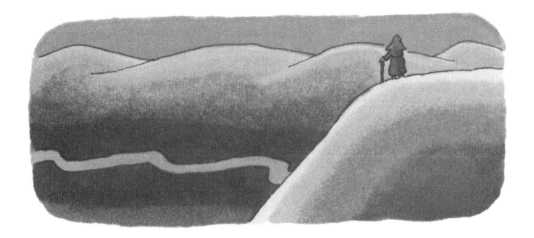

How can a young person live his life purely?
By living the way that your word tells us, surely!
I seek you with all of my heart every day;
let me live by your law and not falter or stray.
I have hidden your word in my heart deep within
to prevent me from failing you, Lord, with my sin.
And I praise you, O Lord; your decrees I have sung.
I repeat them aloud, for they come from your tongue.
I rejoice in obeying, as if I'd found treasure;
to think of your word gives me nothing but pleasure.

Psalm 119

Wise Words to Live By

The fear of the Lord
is where wise men begin;
and the ones who reject it
are quite foolish men.

Proverbs 1:7

Trust in the Father with all of your heart,
not your own understanding; we're never so smart.
And acknowledge his name in whatever you do,
and he'll straighten the pathway that lies before you.

Proverbs 3:5-6

The fear of the Lord will add years to your life,
but your days will be shortened by evil and strife.

Proverbs 10:27

A person of pride
only comes to disgrace,
but the humble gain wisdom
for running the race.

Proverbs 11:2

A gossip repeats every secret he's heard, but a trustworthy person will not say a word.

Proverbs 11:13

A man who won't punish cannot love his child, for in love there is discipline— careful, not wild.

Proverbs 13:24

Diligent work is the pathway to profit;
but he who's just talking gets poverty off it.

Proverbs 14:23

A gentle reply makes
the angry one fly,
but the angrier word
means the anger is stirred.

Proverbs 15:1

A friend will love you
all the time;
and when you're down,
he'll help you climb.
Proverbs 17:17

Support for the poor
is a loan to the Lord,
and will always result
in a godly reward.
Proverbs 19:17

Take heed of advice
and accept what you're told,
and you'll find you have wisdom
one day when you're old.
Proverbs 19:20

A slacker too lazy
for plowing in season
is harvesting nothing
and wonders the reason.
Proverbs 20:4

Train up a child
in the way he should go,
and he'll never depart from it,
as he will grow.
Proverbs 22:6

A fool will let his anger roll;
the wise will keep it in control.
Proverbs 29:11

A noble wife is rare in life
more precious far than gold,
her husband knows and trusting grows,
for he has wealth untold.
Proverbs 31:10-11

A Right Time

All things on earth have a time and a season,
for under God's heaven they all have a reason:

A time when we die and a time for our birth,
a time when we plant or uproot in the earth,
a time when we heal and a time when we hurt,
a time to tear down or to build in the dirt,
a time when we laugh and a time when we weep,
a time when we dance and a time when we sleep,
a time for embracing or staying apart,
a time when we search and a time to lose heart,
a time when we keep or a time when we send,
a time when we tear and a time when we mend,
a time when we speak and a time to be silent,
a time to have peace or for war that is violent.

And how is the worker repaid for his duty?
The Lord has created a world full of beauty;
He planted eternity here in each heart,
and he blessed us immeasurably right from the start.
Ecclesiastes 3

Dry Bones Come to Life

The prophet Ezekiel
walked through a valley,
where ancient battallions
had seen their last rally.
Ezekiel wandered
the field all alone,
and he saw it was filled
with old skull and dry bone.
He thought of his Israel,
both dry and dead,
and he suddenly heard
the Lord's voice as it said,
"All the bones, son of man,
can they live once again?
You will speak to them;
tell them I'll turn them to men."
And Ezekiel spoke
to the bones from the battle;
he heard all the joints
come together and rattle,

and tendons were joined
as they started to mesh,
and were suddenly covered
all over with flesh!
And he saw a great army
with shield and with sword,
as a vision of power
and hope in the Lord,
for he knew that if dry bones
could live once again,
there was hope for his Israel–
as well as all men.

Ezekiel 37

The Fiery Furnace

Shadrach, Meshach,
and Abednego,
were three Israelite
friends many ages ago
who would bow to no kings
or give other gods praise,
for they saved it for God,
and were true to his ways.
So the king was upset,
and he called for that crew,
meaning Shadrach and Meshach
and Abednego, too.
He said, "Bow, or you'll surely
be thrown in the furnace!"
They thought to themselves,
"Would the king really burn us?"
But still, they held out
for the God that is true.
And so Shadrach and Meshach,
Abednego, too,
were taken and thrown
in the furnace's fire—

to think of it now makes a body perspire!
But the King came to see; he opened the door,
and he saw the three prisoners—no, he saw four!
For the fourth was an angel, and all were quite well.
The king was impressed and immediately fell
on his knees, for he knew an adventure this odd
was a sign of the true and the genuine God.
So Shadrach and Meshach, Abednego, three
were removed from the oven; the king set them free.

Daniel 3

Daniel and the Lions

Daniel, each day, said his prayers on his knees
while his window was open, providing a breeze.
But the window let someone—a glum one—look in,
and that someone was one of the king's loyal men.
And he went to the king and told what he knew:
"Oh, your highness, he prays to his God, and not you.
For I passed by his window and that's what I saw,
so he has to be punished for breaking the law."
So they hurried to Daniel, arrested him then:
he was thrown to the lions and left in their den.

But returning next morning,
the king called his name,
and from out of the darkness,
a voice surely came
and said, "I am still here,
for the Lord of all Zion,
sent angels last evening
to soothe every lion."
Each cat was as meek
and as mild as a kitten,
and Daniel sat calmly,
unharmed and unbitten!
The king was so happy
he made a new law:
that the Lord would be held
by the kingdom in awe.
So the lesson of Daniel,
so wise and so true,
is to stand up for God,
and he'll stand up for you.
Daniel 6

Fish Food

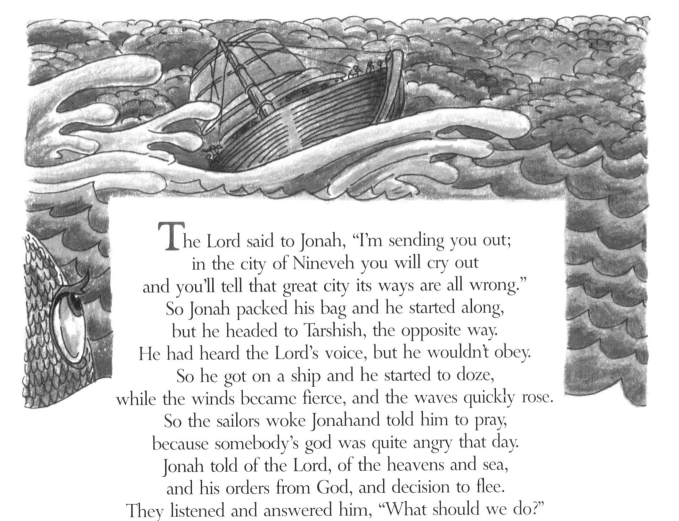

The Lord said to Jonah, "I'm sending you out;
in the city of Nineveh you will cry out
and you'll tell that great city its ways are all wrong."
So Jonah packed his bag and he started along,
but he headed to Tarshish, the opposite way.
He had heard the Lord's voice, but he wouldn't obey.
So he got on a ship and he started to doze,
while the winds became fierce, and the waves quickly rose.
So the sailors woke Jonahand told him to pray,
because somebody's god was quite angry that day.
Jonah told of the Lord, of the heavens and sea,
and his orders from God, and decision to flee.
They listened and answered him, "What should we do?"

"Throw me off, for he's angry with me, not you."
So they threw the poor prophet right over the side,
and as soon as they did, the wind slowly died.
But for Jonah, catastrophe certainly followed:
a fish saw him floating, and swam up and swallowed!
He stayed in its stomach three nights and three days.
When a man is in trouble, he thinks and he prays,
so the prophet cried out from a fish to the Lord,
and admitted he'd failed, he had gone overboard.
So the Lord pitied Jonah and gave a command,
and the fish spit the prophet upon the dry land.
He hurried to Nineveh, quick to obey,
for when God gives an order, we shouldn't delay!

The Book of Jonah

The New Testament

Mary and the Angel

An Angel appeared
to young Mary one day,
and she trembled in fear,
as he started to say,
"You rejoice and be happy,
for God is with you!
Do not be afraid,
for He's pleased with you, too.
You will soon be expecting
a new baby son,
and his name will be Jesus,
the holiest one,

and the Father will place him on David's great throne,
and he'll rule it forever and call us his own."
"But I'm just a young girl, and a soon-to-be bride!" So
the Lord will protect you," the angel replied. And the
girl showed her faith: "May it be as you say,
for I'm serving the Lord, and I always obey."

Luke 1

The First Christmas

A census was taken of every man's worth,
calling men to return to the town of their birth,
and so Joseph brought Mary to Bethlehem town
(where their greatest king, David, had come to his crown),
and, arriving, they wanted to sleep at an inn,
but the place was too crowded, with travelling men,

so Mary and Joseph in Bethlehem slept
in a crude little stable, where cattle are kept.
But that evening the time came, and Mary gave birth;
the promised Messiah had come to the earth.
She wrapped him and put him to sleep in a manger,
a trough—but a bed for a heavenly stranger.

Luke 2

The Shepherds

Some shepherds were watching their flocks in the field,
when a messenger angel of God was revealed;
the heavenly light only filled them with fear,
but he told them, "Don't worry, good tidings are here!
There is joy for all people that live on the earth,
for today our own savior, the Christ, has his birth.
And you'll find him in Bethlehem where he's at rest;
in a manger he sleeps, and in cloth he is dressed."

And the angel was suddenly
joined by a throng,
who appeared in the night,
praising God with their song:
singing, "Glory to God,
in the highest above,
and on earth, there is peace,
among those in his love."
When the angels had left them,
the shepherds decided,
"Let's go now to see
what the angel confided."
They hurried and found
the small child in the manger,
and left telling others,
each friend and each stranger,
of angels and Jesus,
their wonderful story;
they kept praising God,
and proclaiming his glory.
Luke 2

Lost at the Temple

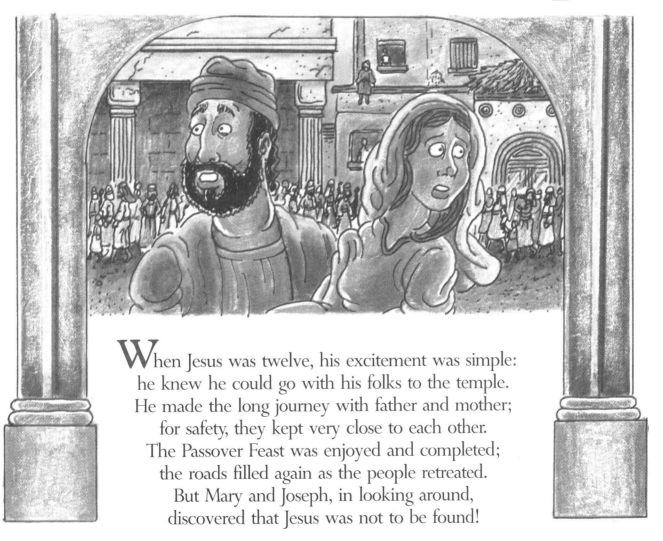

When Jesus was twelve, his excitement was simple:
he knew he could go with his folks to the temple.
He made the long journey with father and mother;
for safety, they kept very close to each other.
The Passover Feast was enjoyed and completed;
the roads filled again as the people retreated.
But Mary and Joseph, in looking around,
discovered that Jesus was not to be found!

To the city they hurried, and searched everywhere,
and at last, in the temple, they spotted him there
with the scribes and the teachers, discussing the Word;
The teachers were shocked at the wisdom they heard!
But his parents said, "Jesus, you filled us with fear!"
"But I work for my Father, you knew I'd be here."
His answer befuddled his parents that day,
but he loved both his folks and would always obey.
He grew to be wise as he grew in his size,
and by men and the Lord he was loved and adored.

Luke 2

Jesus and John

A man in the wilderness, preaching of sin,
was attracting great masses of women and men.
He baptized with water to show they were clean
when the Lord washed away what was evil or mean.
But when Jesus approached, he said, "Lord, can't you see
that it's backwards, for you should be baptizing me!"
But when Jesus insisted, his friend put him under,
and afterward, John saw the sky torn asunder!
The Spirit came down in the form of a dove,
and a voice said, "Behold my true Son whom I love."
And the people knew Jesus was truly God's Son,
the Messiah long promised, the Lord's chosen one.

Matthew 3

Jesus is Tempted

Jesus went into
the desert one day
for some time with the Lord
and to fast and to pray.
He was there forty days
and ate nothing at all,
so one morning,
the devil himself came to call.
He said, "If you're real,
you can make the stones bread."
"We depend on the Word,
not just food," Jesus said.
So the devil took Jesus
up high on the temple.
"Just jump, let the angels
come save you, it's simple."
And Jesus said,
"Don't put your God to the test."
But the devil would not
let the Son of God rest;
they went to a mountain
and saw everything.

"It is yours," Satan said, "if you'll call me your king."
"Get away," Jesus answered, "we worship God only."
The devil then left him, but he wasn't lonely,
for angels were sent to take care of him then;
he'd been tested and tempted, but sin didn't win,
for whenever the devil's temptations occurred,
he was strong and he quoted the truth from God's Word.

Matthew 4

Jesus and the Disciples

Jesus was walking along by the sea
and invited two brothers, "Come on, follow me,
and I'll teach you to fish, not for food, but for men."
They put down their nets and they followed him then.
A collector of taxes abandoned his booth;
he was following Jesus, to learn about truth.

There were men of all kinds who received Jesus' call,
and became his disciples—a dozen in all.
So they travelled with Jesus wherever he went,
and he gave them his lessons and told what they meant.

Disciples of Jesus, remember their names:
Bartholomew, Matthew, and Thomas, and James;
there were Philip, and Andrew, and Peter, his brother,
and Simon the Zealot, and James (yes, another),
and Judas and John. These eleven obeyed him,
but Judas Iscariot sadly betrayed him.

Matthew 4

The Lord's Prayer

Jesus was teaching his friends about praying and said we should pray to our Father by saying,

"Our Father in heaven, the holiest One,
your kingdom is coming; your will may be done
on earth as in heaven, and feed us each day,
and forgive us our debts; we forgive the same way;
don't let us be tempted, but keep us from sin.
For your kingdom, and power, and glory. Amen."

Matthew 6

Walk on the Water

Jesus' friends took a boat in the night,
but the wind started whipping them left, and then right.
The Disciples were rowing with all of their might,
when they spotted a figure come into their sight!
He was walking on waves: was the figure a ghost?
But it looked more like Jesus, their heavenly host
who had strolled to their boat from the opposite coast,
and the group was excited, but Peter the most.

"If you're Jesus," he called, "Let me walk out to you."
He went over the side and deserted his crew;
He walked on the water a moment, it's true,
but he thought of the storm, and his fear quickly grew.

And so Peter fell in, and went under a wave,
but his master was present, to seek and to save;
the disciple had stumbled, but still he was brave,
for he stepped out on faith with the power God gave.

Matthew 14

Jesus and the Children

Jesus was teaching and preaching the Word,
to a crowd when a wonderful moment occurred.
The parents were bringing their girls and their boys
to be close to the teacher and share in his joys.
The disciples were trying to turn them away;
But he turned when he saw it, and spoke up to say,
"Let the children approach me, don't hinder them, please,
for the kingdom of God is for children like these."

Mark 10

A Little Man in a Tree

Old Zacchaeus, rich and small:
 hardly any friends at all,
 taking taxes, cheating men
until the day he turned from sin.
For Jesus came to town one day,
and people watched him make his way.
 Zacchaeus was too short to see;
 he climbed the branches of a tree
 and Jesus then looked up to say,

"I'm coming to your house today!"
Zacchaeus thought, "Could he mean me?
The sinner in the sycamore tree?"
The people grumbled. "He's a sinner!
Jesus can't go there for dinner!"
"I have stolen, Lord," said Zack,
"But that, times four, I'll give them back!"
He turned from sin, despite the cost,
for Jesus seeks and saves the lost.
Luke 19

How To Be Saved

Nicodemus came at night,
to Jesus, in the soft moonlight and said,
"I know that God sent you, because of miracles you do."
And Jesus said, "Be born again, for that's the only hope for men.
God loves the world! He sent his son
to bring this life to everyone. Believe in him,
and never die. He loves you!
That's the reason why."

John 3

Jesus the Healer

When people met Jesus,
they knew he was real,
for when people were sick,
he would lovingly heal.
He would make the blind see
and the mute learn to talk,
as the deaf learned to hear
and the lame learned to walk.
They brought him a man
in a paralyzed state,
but they couldn't see Jesus:
the crowd was too great.

So they went to the roof and they opened a section,
and lowered the patient in Jesus' direction.
The master instructed, "Get up! Get your mat,
and go home," and he healed him, as simple as that.
Whether silent or deaf, with no eyesight or lame,
they were healed and were joyful and praising his name.

Mark 2

The Good Samaritan

Jesus told a parable
(a simple tale that's sharable)
about a man who made a trip,
but found himself in robbers' grip.
They beat him up, and left him lying
in the road, close to dying.
Soon there came a stately priest,
and did he help? Not in the least.

A Levite came along that way,
and walked on, too, without delay.
But someone from Samaria
(a much-avoided area)
came by, and felt the strongest pity,
took him to the nearest city,
left him at a fine hotel,
and paid the way to make him well.
And when we stop to do the same,
we glorify our Savior's name.

Luke 10

The Last Supper

Jesus found a quiet upper room,
and used it for his final supper room.
Disciples shared the wine and broke the bread,
"Remember me like this," their Master said.
For Jesus knew he'd have to leave his friends,
to fix a feast above that never ends.

Matthew 26

The Cross

Jesus taught the world of God above;
he healed, and fed, and spread his Father's love.
He did the will of God for all his days,
but there were some who didn't like his ways.
They waited for the time to be just right,
and came to capture Jesus in the night.
They held a trial, accused him with a lie,
and quickly ruled that Jesus had to die.
He heard his sentence silently, and still,
took up his cross and hauled it to a hill.

The women wept; disciples hid in fright;
and Jesus hung in pain that Friday night.
He honored God until his final breath,
forgiving those who brought about his death.
The sky grew dark as Jesus breathed his last;
he said, "It's finished," then his spirit passed.
They took him down and put him in a tomb.
And those who loved him hung their heads in gloom.
But he would soon return, alive and well,
the happy news we live and love to tell!

John 19

He Lives!

In the tomb, Jesus rested three bitter days,
but when Sunday arrived with its first morning rays,
Mary Magdalene faithfully came to the site
and discovered the stone had been moved overnight!
So she told the disciples that Jesus was gone,
and a pair of them hurried there: Peter and John.
There was nothing inside but the burial clothes;
could it be that their crucified teacher arose?

But his friend, Mary Magdalene, started to cry,
and two angels, in white, asked the weeping one why.
"They have taken my Lord, and I don't know just where."
And she turned and saw Jesus was standing right there!
And he said to her, "Mary, now go tell my brothers."
She ran to his friends, and disciples, and others,
and told them that Jesus had risen today.
We still tell the news, in the same joyful way.

John 20

The Great Commission

When Jesus returned to his Father's right hand,
he provided his friends with a final command:
"In all heaven and earth I've been given the power,
so go to the nations, beginning this hour,
proclaiming the gospel to all who will hear it;
you speak for the Father, and Son, and the Spirit.
So baptize them, teaching them all to obey
the commands I have given you, day after day.

You will start in Jerusalem, then to Samaria,
then to the ends of the earth–every area.
God's Holy Spirit will give you the power,
and I will be there with you always, each hour."
He vanished from sight as he rose in the air,
but he lives in our hearts, and he'll always be there.

Matthew 28

Power from Above

A church without Jesus? It never could be!
For the Lord sent his Spirit to guide you and me.
The disciples were gathered on Pentecost day,
when the sound of a cyclone came rushing their way.
As the noise and commotion grew higher and higher,
they saw what appeared to be tongues of real fire!
The Spirit was filling each heart with his love,
and providing the power that comes from above.
The disciples were ready to cover the earth,
as the Church celebrated the day of its birth.

Acts 2

Saul Meets Jesus

Saul hated Christians,
and he sought to have
each one pursued and caught.
He'd search each village, town, or city,
root them out, and show no pity.
Christians feared him worst of all
but God had other plans for Saul.
So to Damascus Saul was bound
when light from heaven flashed around.

It knocked him down and stole his sight;
a voice said, "Saul, give up your fight.
It's Jesus; I'm the one you're seeking."
And the Lord continued speaking,
sending Saul, despite his blindness,
to a man, who full of kindness,
helped restore to Saul his sight,
but Saul had truly seen the light.
His heart had heard
a higher call,
and God renamed his servant Paul.

Acts 9

Paul the Missionary

He walked the roads and sailed the sea,
to bring the Word to you and me.
On foot or via sailing ships,
he toured the world in three great trips
and started churches all around
by telling of the love he'd found.
And when he had to sit in jail,
he taught the churches through the mail.
He spread the news across the world,
and wouldn't stop when stones were hurled,

or when his Roman ship was wrecked;
he only won the world's respect.
His letters tell of Jesus Christ,
and why Christ's life was sacrificed
to wash away our human sin,
and how he rose to live again,
so those who love him never die.
This letter writer tells us why,
and through him we can hear the call
of Christ, who sent the man named Paul.

Acts 13

Words for Living

Here is how you know God's love is true:
we sinned, yet Jesus Christ has died for you.
Romans 5:8

When we don't know how we should pray,
the Spirit knows just what to say.
Romans 8:26

If we love God the way we should,
he uses all things for our good.
Romans 8:28

We know it's very true, and very simple:
The Spirit lives in you, and you're his temple!
1 Corinthians 3:16

The body is one, and we're each just a part:
an ear, or a tongue, or a toe, or a heart.
You might be a foot, and I might be a hand,
but the head will be Christ and we're his to command.

1 Corinthians 12

Love is patient; love is kind;
it doesn't seek a fault to find.
It doesn't envy, isn't proud,
or angry, boastful, rude, or loud.
It trusts, and hopes, and saves the day,
for love will never pass away.

1 Corinthians 13

The fruit of the Spirit is love, joy, and peace,
while our patience and kindness will also increase.
You are faithful, and gentle; we show self-control,
if the Spirit of Christ is at home in your soul.

Galatians 5

Be strong in the Lord and in his mighty power;
the armor of God will protect you each hour.
The belt that is truth and the breastplate of right,
and the shield of your faith will prevail in the fight.
Salvation, your helmet; the sword of the Spirit
is God's holy Word, and the devil will fear it!

Ephesians 6

Rejoice in the Lord, and I'll say it again:
rejoice, and be gentle to women and men.
You needn't be anxious; just share it in prayer,
as you thank him and give him your burdens to bear.
And the peace of our God, which we can't understand,
will be guarding your heart and your mind, in his hand.

Philippians 4

Consider it joy when you're facing a trial,
for the Lord is maturing your faith all the while.

James 1

Be quick to listen, slow to speak,
and slow to anger (don't be weak!).

James 1

Do what the Word says, don't just sit there and hear it,
deceiving yourselves, but not fooling the Spirit.

James 1

This is the message: God is our light.
No darkness is in him, and so we do right.

1 John 1

Let's love one another, it comes from above;
it shows we're his children, for God is our love.

1 John 4

Christ Will Come Again!

The Lord has made his revelation, making clear to every nation,
history is just his story, reveal the Christ to every eye.
When things of earth at last grow dim, we'll join the Lord, and live with him.
He'll wipe away our tears, and then we'll worship as he reigns. Amen!

Revelation 1